# SOMALIA

## "BLACK HAWK DOWN"
### My Missionary Mission turned Military Mission
### By
### Harvey Carroll, Jr.
### (THE UNELECTED PRESIDENT)

This is my fifth book; and a near 30 page Poem and a Book on "Desert Storm." Books include a Mini-Autobiography "THE UNELECTED PRSIDENT), SCREWED, which is about the Lewinsky sex scandal and my involvement in Clinton's "Little White House Lie," and my "Operation Just Cause;"my suggestion for the Panama Invasion...

I intend to publish a series of Books under the trademark
"THE UNELECTED PRESIDENT"

**ISBN-13: 978-1530078981**

**ISBN-10: 1530078989**

# CONTENTS

# INTRODUCTION

In this book you will find that "Black Hawk Down" the movie was really a total screw up. Granted it was a good War film, if it had not been based upon a real story, "my story."

You will come to understand that I had suggested a missionary mission into Somalia that got turned into a military mission; hence "Black Hawk Down." I made the suggestions with old Bush, Sr. Administration "Intelligence Contacts" that I had since making suggestions for the Panama Invasion "Operation Just Cause" (also a bit of overkill), and me helping to organize and maintain the multinational coalition during the 1st Gulf War "Operation Desert Storm" (The 100 Hour War).

I ask why we can't have a "New Earth Army" that heals instead of kills.

# DEDICATION

*This book is dedicated to those working with The United Nations and Global Citizens that work daily paid and unpaid to help develop constructive policy, provide leadership for worthy projects that continue to further humanities best interest.*

*This is also dedicated to those that provided service in Somalia and those that paid the ultimate sacrifice after the shift of policy from a missionary mission into a military mission... My commonsense prevail in future policymaking...............*

# 1
# SOMALIA
# My "MISSIONARY MISSION"

*Somalia was a policy that ended up being depressive for me. I was trying to do something good by creating a missionary mission to feed people.*

*My simple suggestion to feed those in need ended up being converted from a missionary mission into a military mission that cost over three thousand Somali lives and 12 U.S. Soldiers Lives[1]. Not a good feeling to deal with for over a decade when I just wanted to feed a few people.*

*Supplying AID and winning the hearts and minds of Africans. This thought started with a date and long café' discussion with a girl while I was in the Arm, stationed in West German.*

---

[1] MOVIE credits; "Black Hawk Down"

*I still remembered our deep and intimate conversations years later after I was elected as Vice President of a campus club at Eastern Kentucky University called CIRUNA (Council on International Relations and United Nation Affairs).*

*The President of the club was a former Somali Diplomat to Great Briton and Canada. His name was Hashi, and he and I became pretty good friends. We did some public speaking forums on International Relations, International Terrorism and other foreign policy concerns.*

*Hashi and I made the Richmond Register newspaper discussing International Terrorism on Tuesday September the 23, 1986 in which I noted on page 69 and 70 of this book but I will point out the front page again that list my Somali collogue.*[2]

---

[2] Richmond Register news paper on Tuesday September the 23, 1986.

# The Richmond Register

## Founded 1917–Home of Eastern Kentucky University

No. 228          Richmond, Kentucky 40475          Tuesday, September 23, 1986          10 Pag

## Experts discuss terrorism at forum

By GEORGE FERRELL
Register Staff Writer

RICHMOND — The Council for International Relations and the United Nations Association held a public forum Monday night, providing time for four speakers to give their views on the topic of international terrorism.

Among those speaking were Dr. Robert Bagby, an EKU professor of Law Enforcement who teaches a course on terrorism; Dr. Ralph Fretty, EKU professor of government; Abdulkadir A. Hashi, a former Somali diplomat who has served in England and Canada; and Harvey Carroll Jr., a student and Estill County native formerly involved in anti-terrorism work in Europe.

Bagby, in opening the lectures, gave students an overview of the reasons for terrorism. These include, according to Bagby, class and social structure, ethnic backgrounds, religion, ideology, sectarian, and irredentist (recovery of territory now under a foreign government).

Terrorist attacks have increased 10-fold during the last decade, according to Bagby, with the majority of the activity occurring in Great Britain, West Germany, Spain, Japan, Italy, France and the Middle East.

Pointing out that terrorists are their "own artists," Bagby said the West is open to attack due to personal freedoms and the ideals of democracy.

"The West is vulnerable to attack because we have certain standards and beliefs that make it that way," Bagby said.

Lack of unity and weakness, such as the American inability to bring economic sanctions against Libya earlier this year can give terrorists an open season, according to Bagby, who said he supported the mid-April bombing of Libya.

About 70 percent of all terrorist activity involves the use of explosives, with the term Improvised Explosive Devices (IED) being applied to that use.

There are many terrorist organizations, some lasting for hours and others for decades, according to Bagby.

"Picture a book this thick," Bagby said, indicating a large book. "And you would not have them all."

Some of the key groups around the world include the Palestinian Liberation Organization (PLO), the Armenian ASLA, the Baeder Meinhof Gang (W. Germany), the Red Brigade (Italy), and the

(Please see Experts on Page 2)

Dr. Ralph Fretty (standing) lectured during last night's forum on international terrorism held in the Kennamer Room of the Powell Building on the EKU campus last night. Fretty, as a professor of government, gave a perspective on the origins and causes of terrorism. Seated is Dr. Robert Bagby, a professor of law enforcement involved in teaching a regular course offering through the law enforcement department (Register photo by George Ferrell).

*The Diplomat and I discussed a variety of economic topics concerning his home land of Somalia, and the declining fate and hunger of Somalia.*

3

*The empathetic views that he shared with me about Somali reminded me of an old girlfriend from Europe that I used to discuss African politics with and that felt the U.S. and Western Europe could do more to assist…*

*▓▓▓▓▓▓▓ was a very beautiful and brilliant lady that I talked about in other chapters; whereby she referred to how the Soviet Union was winning the hearts and minds of the African Nations by providing economic aid. Nearly a decade later that statement along with Hashi's diplomatic sharing of his empathetic experiences.*

*Hashi's first hand views on Somalia shaped my opinion and I wanted to help Somalia by using such concepts. Also, America was facing economic problems and the gloom and doom rhetoric was over exaggerated in many ways during the political season that was starting to ramp up…*

*I felt that it might be news worthy to show that the United States wasn't doing so bad compared to other 3rd world countries that had citizens starving by the masses on a daily basis.*

*So once again I called my Washington, D.C. based Intelligence Agent contact and suggested that the United States should supply Aid to Somalia.*

*I suggested that it be sold by having the press corps waiting on the coast as the troops came to shore and this is exactly what happened...*

*Talking points related to poverty in other less developed countries... The suggestion was made with the hope that this would not damage the constructive thinking within America. Granted we had debt and deficit problems, but we were far from third world...*

*Verbatim text from Wikipedia link https://en.wikipedia.org/wiki/Battle_of_Mogadishu_(1993)#Mission_shift*

"<u>Operation Provide Relief</u> began in August 1992, when the U.S. President <u>George H. W. Bush</u> announced that U.S. military transports would support the multinational U.N. relief effort in Somalia. Ten <u>C-130s</u> and 400 people were deployed to <u>Mombasa</u>, Kenya, airlifting aid to Somalia's remote areas and reducing reliance on truck convoys. One member of the 86th Supply Squadron, <u>USAFE</u>'s only contribution to the operation, was deployed with the ground support contingent. The C-130s delivered 48,000 tons of food and medical supplies in six months to international humanitarian organizations trying to help Somalia's more than three million starving people."

# 2
# SOMALIA
# STRATEGIC DEFENSE
# AND SHIPPING ROUTE

*Somalia is a very strategic defense location to respond to threats from Africa and/or the Middle East. Somalia is also a key area for shipping routes. Often there is Pirates from Somalia that prey upon ships passing along the Somalia coast.*

*I'll get into how U.S./U.N. bases could greatly enhance not only defense, shipping, but also the 3D's (Diplomacy, Democracy and Development later in this book. For now I wish to get into what I was thinking back when I made the suggestions to supply AID to Somalia...*

*There were a couple other reasons why I thought supplying Aid to Somalia was a good idea. During "Desert Storm" Saddam tried to enlist/hire soldiers from the "War-Lords" of Somalia. I assume that they were hungry and desperate and* willing to participate in the suicidal venture. Somalia is in a very strategic shipping route that was vital to oil and gas shipping from the Middle East. While it had not became an issue at that time we later became aware of the Somali Pirate operations that threatened the shipping routes.

I felt that a missionary mission was necessary to help not only their country, but the Untied States as well. I liked the idea of winning their hearts and mind; by showing that this country has a heart and it was capable of compassion. This was a very huge shift from the destruction and death that was caused in the 1st Gulf War.

It was also an election year, and I felt that it could show Americans that even though the United States has had a bit of an economic slowdown that it was in great shape compared to those third world countries. That in actuality, our nation was doing wonderful in comparison to others in the world.

*Unfortunately President Bush didn't articulate that message very well even though he had a prime opportunity to counter President Clintons "It's the Economy Stupid" campaign slogan presented by Consultant James Carville.*

# 3
# COMMANDER N CHIEF CLINTON ("BLACK HAWK DOWN")

*The entire Bush campaign was around his successes as Commander n Chief. Clinton wisely focused on his consultant James Carville's theme "It's the economy stupid." Clinton's campaign was ultimately successful and he became the new Commander n Chief...*

*The American people and I really worried about Clinton's ability to manage military affairs. I remember as starting a rumor during the Presidential Campaign that Clinton got his foreign policy experience at the "International House of Pancakes".*

*After Clinton was elected for obvious reasons, my contacts were somewhat "Black Listed" and no longer had access to White House Policymaking; therefore, I was worried that policies in Iraq and Somalia could begin to fail...*

*I had just helped organize and maintain the multinational coalition during the 1st Gulf war "Operation Desert Storm" that was extremely successful. In general the Air campaign was 37 days if I remember correctly and the war its self I had sold as "The 100 Hour War." Only 4 days, 4 hours and we called it a day with Saddam's army nearly destroyed he gave up.*

*But, now Clinton is the Commander n Chief and I was seeing issues in Iraq and a shift towards military thinking Somalia. Somalia was never supposed to be an AID operation…*

*In Iraq we only needed to contain Saddam as he was diminished in power to little more than the Mayor of Baghdad, and in Somalia we just needed to be a feeding station… Simple enough right? A high school kid could handle this…*

*Clinton screws it up very quickly. In Iraq he allows Saddam to attack Kurds* in the north. In Somalia General Garrison converts the missionary mission into a Military Mission; hence, **"Black Hawk Down."**

*Verbatim text from Wikipedia link…*
*https://en.wikipedia.org/wiki/Battle_of_Mogadishu_(1993)*

*"The **Battle of Mogadishu** or **Day of the Rangers** (Somali: Maalintii Rangers), was part of Operation Gothic Serpent and was fought on the 3rd and 4 October 1993, in Mogadishu, Somalia, between forces of the United States, supported by UNOSOM II, and Somali militiamen loyal to the self-proclaimed president-to-be Mohamed Farrah Aidid, who had support from armed civilian fighters. The battle is also referred to as the **First Battle of Mogadishu** to distinguish it from subsequent battles in that city, such as*

*the Second Battle of Mogadishu of 2006.*

*The initial U.S. Joint Special Operations force, Task Force Ranger, was a collaboration of various elite special forces units from Army Special Operations Command, Air Force Special Operations Command andNavy Special Warfare Command. Task Force Ranger was dispatched to seize two of Aidid's high-echelon lieutenants during a meeting in the city. The goal of the operation was achieved, though conditions spiraled into the deadly Battle of Mogadishu. The initial operation of 3 October 1993, intended to last an hour, became an overnight standoff and rescue operation extending into daylight hours of 4 October."*

*I strongly disagreed with the shift of policy towards a military mission. I felt it was necessary to maintain neutrality to meet the constitutionality side of the AID mission.*

*Verbatim text from Wikipedia link...* *https://en.wikipedia.org/wiki/Battle_ of_Mogadishu_(1993)#Mission_shift*

**"Mission shift[edit]**

UNOSOM II humvee departing for the seaport of Mogadishu.

*On 3 March 1993, the U.N. Secretary-General Boutros Boutros-Ghali submitted to the U.N. Security Council his recommendations for effecting the transition from UNITAF to UNOSOM II. He indicated that since Resolution 794's adoption in December 1992, UNITAF's presence and operations had created a positive impact on Somalia's security situation and on the effective delivery of humanitarian assistance (UNITAF deployed some 37,000 personnel over forty percent of southern and central Somalia). However, there was still no effective government, police, or national army with the result of serious security threats to U.N. personnel. To that end, the Security Council authorized UNOSOM II to establish a secure environment throughout Somalia, to achieve national reconciliation so as to create a democratic state.*[21][22]

*At the Conference on National Reconciliation in Somalia, held on 15 March 1993, in Addis Ababa, Ethiopia, all fifteen Somali parties agreed to the terms set out to restore peace and democracy. Yet, by May it became clear that, although a signatory to the March*

Agreement, <u>Mohammed      Farrah Aidid</u>'s faction would not cooperate in         the         Agreement's implementation.[21]

Aidid began to broadcast anti-U.N.    propaganda    on    Radio Mogadishu after believing that the U.N.       was       purposefully marginalizing him in an attempt to "rebuild    Somalia".    Lieutenant General <u>Çevik Bir</u> ordered the radio station shut down, in an attempt to quash the beginning of what could turn into a rebellion. Civilian spies throughout      UNOSOM      II's headquarters    likely    led    to    the uncovering of the U.N.'s plan. Aidid ordered SNA militia to attack a Pakistani force on 5 June 1993, that had been tasked with the inspection of an arms cache located at the radio station, possibly out of fear that this was a task force sent to shut down the broadcast. The result was 24 dead, and 57 wounded Pakistani troops, as well as 1 wounded Italian and 3 wounded American soldiers. On 6 June 1993, the U.N. Security Council passed _Resolution 837_, for the arrest and prosecution of the persons responsible for the death and wounding of the peacekeepers.[23]

On 12 June, U.S. troops started attacking targets in Mogadishu in hopes of finding Aidid, a campaign which lasted until 16 June. On 17 June, a $25,000 _warrant_ was issued by _Admiral Jonathan Howe_ for information leading to Aidid's arrest, but he was never captured.[24] Howe also requested a _counter-terrorist_ rescue force after the Pakistanis' deaths.

### Attack on safe house[edit]

On 12 July 1993, a U.S.-led operation was launched on what was believed to be a safe house where Aidid was hiding in Mogadishu. During the 17-minute combat operation, U.S. _Cobra_ attack helicopters fired 16 _TOW_ _missiles_ and thousands of 20-millimeter cannon rounds into the compound, killing 60 people. However, the number of Somali fatalities was disputed. _Abdi Qeybdiid_, Aidid's interior minister, claimed 73 dead, including women and children who had been in the safe house. The reports _Jonathan Howe_ got after the attack placed the number of dead at 20, all men. The International Committee of the Red Cross set the number of dead at 54.[25] Aidid was not present.

The operation would lead to the deaths of four journalists – _Dan Eldon_, Hos Maina, Hansi Kraus and Anthony Macharia – who were killed by angry Mogadishu mobs when they arrived to cover the incident,[26] which presaged the Battle of Mogadishu.[27]

Some believe that this American attack was a turning point in unifying Somalis against U.S. efforts in Somalia, including former *moderates and those opposed to the Habar Gidir.[28][29]*

### Task Force Ranger[edit]

*Bravo Company, 3rd Battalion of the 75th Ranger Regiment in Somalia, 1993.*

*On 8 August 1993, Aidid's militia detonated a remote controlled bomb against a U.S. military vehicle, killing four soldiers. Two weeks later another bomb injured seven more.[30] In response, U.S. President Bill Clinton approved the proposal to deploy a special task force composed of elite special forces units, including 400 U.S.*

*Army Rangers and Delta Force operators.*[31]

*On 22 August, the unit deployed to Somalia under the command of* <u>Major General William F. Garrison</u>*, commander of the special multi-disciplinary* <u>Joint Special Operations Command</u> *(JSOC) at the time.*

*The force consisted of:*

- *B Company, 3rd Battalion, 75th Ranger Regiment*
- *C Squadron, 1st Special Forces Operational Detachment-Delta (1st SFOD-D)*
- *A deployment package of 16 helicopters and personnel from the 160th Special Operations Aviation Regiment (160th SOAR), which included MH-60 Black Hawks and AH/MH-6 Little Birds.*
- *Navy SEALs from the Naval Special Warfare Development Group (DEVGRU)*

- *Air Force Pararescuemen and Combat Controllers from the 24th Special Tactics Squadron.*[32]

*On 21 September, Task Force Ranger captured Aidid's financier, Osman Ali Atto.*

**First Black Hawk shot down**

*At around 02:00 on 25 September, Aidid's men shot down a 101st Airborne Division Black Hawk with an RPG and killed three crew members at New Port near Mogadishu. The shootdown was a huge SNA psychological victory."*

*The special-ops blunder somewhat substantiated the rumor that I started on Clinton during the Bush's campaign where*

*Somalia*[3] *engagement may have been justified via the U.N. and constitutionally;*

---

[3] Harvey Carroll, Jr. "Bush Administration Policy that may have came about when I suggested supplying Aid to Somalia

*however, we started out providing missionary type aid and we should have stuck with that plan... The policy changed from being a missionary mission to a military mission and chaos and terrorism has been on the rise in the region because of the shift in mission...*

*Granted a week case could be made that it was to protect Americans abroad. I remember thinking that the commanders may have undermined the constitution by placing servicemen in danger; thereby, provoking conflict instead of maintaining the original justification of supplying aid.*

*The shift from missionary to military mission was obviously irresponsible and it got Americans Servicemen killed.*

because, I had became friends with (Hashi) a former Somali Diplomat to Great Briton and Canada." (Hashi association Article available by request).

*Verbatim text from Wikipedia link https://en.wikipedia.org/wiki/Battle_ of_Mogadishu_(1993)#Mission_shif t*

*"Aftermath*

*After the battle, the bodies of several of the conflict's U.S. casualties (Black Hawk Super 64's crewmembers and their defenders, Delta Force soldiers MSG Gordon and SFC Shughart) were dragged through Mogadishu's streets by crowds of local civilians and SNA forces.[55] Through negotiation and threats to the Habr Gidr clan leaders by ambassador Robert B. Oakley, all the bodies were eventually recovered. The bodies were returned in poor condition, one with a severed head. Michael Durant was released after 11 days of captivity. On the beach near the base, a memorial was held for those who were killed in combat.[56]*

*Known casualties*
*Pakistan*

*A Pakistani UNOSOM armed convoy making the rounds.*

*A Pakistani soldier was killed and two Pakistanis were wounded during the rescue attempt and assault.[57][verification needed]*

*Malaysia*
*Lance Corporal Mat Aznan Awang was an 18 year old soldier of the 19th Battalion, Royal Malay Regiment of the Malaysian Army (posthumously promoted to Corporal). Driving a Malaysian Condor armoured personnel carrier, he was killed when his vehicle was hit by an RPG on 3 October.[35] Corporal Mat Aznan Awang was awarded the Seri Pahlawan Gagah Perkasa medal (Gallant Warrior/Warrior of Extreme Valor).[40][58]*

*Somalia*

*Ambassador Robert B. Oakley, the U.S. special representative to Somalia, is quoted as saying: "My own personal estimate is that there must have been 1,500 to 2,000 Somalis killed and wounded that day, because that battle was a true battle. And the Americans and those who came to their rescue, were being shot at from all sides ... a deliberate war battle, if you will, on the part of the Somalis. And women and children were being used as shields and some cases women and children were actually firing weapons, and were coming from all sides. Sort of a rabbit warren of huts, houses, alleys, and twisting and turning streets, so those who were trying to defend themselves were shooting back in all directions. Helicopter gun ships were being used as well as all sorts of automatic weapons on the ground by the U.S. and the United Nations. The Somalis, by and large, were* using automatic rifles and grenade launchers and it was a very nasty fight, as intense as almost any battle you would find."[59]

Reliable estimates place the number of Somali insurgents killed at between 800 to as many as 1,000 with perhaps another 4,000 wounded. Somali militants, however, claimed a much lower casualty rate.[60] Aidid himself claimed that only 315 – civilians and militia – were killed and 812 wounded.[6] Captain Haad, in an interview on American public television, said 133 of the SNA militia were killed.[8]

United States
Name Age Action Medal
Operators of 1st Special Forces Operational Detachment-Delta

*MSG Gary Ivan Gordon 33*
*Killed defending Super Six-Four's crew Medal of Honor, Purple Heart[35]*

*SFC Randy Shughart 35*
*Killed defending Super Six-Four's crew Medal of Honor, Purple Heart[35]*

*SSG Daniel D. Busch 25*
*Crashed on Super Six-One, mortally wounded defending the downed crew Silver Star, Purple Heart[58]*

*SFC Earl Robert Fillmore, Jr. 28 Killed moving to the first crash site Silver Star, Purple Heart[61]*

*MSG Timothy "Griz" Lynn Martin 38 Mortally wounded by an RPG on the Lost Convoy, died while en route to a field hospital in GermanySilver Star, Purple Heart.[62][63]*

*Soldiers of the 3rd Ranger Battalion, 75th Ranger Regiment*

*CPL James "Jamie" E. Smith 21 Killed around crash site one Bronze Star Medal with Valor Device and Oak leaf cluster, Purple Heart[64]*

*SPC James M. Cavaco 26 Killed on the Lost Convoy Bronze Star with Valor Device, Purple Heart[65]*

*SGT James Casey Joyce 24 Killed on the Lost Convoy Bronze Star with Valor Device, Purple Heart[65]*

*CPL Richard "Alphabet" W. Kowalewski, Jr. 20 Killed on the Lost Convoy by an RPG Bronze Star with Valor Device, Purple Heart[66]*

*SGT Dominick M. Pilla 21 Killed on Struecker's convoy Bronze Star with Valor Device, Purple Heart[66]*

*SGT Lorenzo M. Ruiz 27 Mortally wounded on the Lost Convoy, died en route to a field hospital in Germany Bronze*

*Star with Valor Device, Purple Heart[66]*

*Pilots and Crew of the 160th Special Operations Aviation Regiment*

*SSG William "Wild Bill" David Cleveland, Jr. 34*

*Crew chief on Super Six-Four, killed Silver Star,*

*Bronze Star,*

*Air Medal with Valor Device, Purple Heart[67]*

*SSG Thomas "Tommie" J. Field 25 Crew chief on Super Six-Four, killed Silver Star,*

*Bronze Star,*

*Air Medal with Valor Device, Purple Heart*

*CW4 Raymond "Ironman" A. Frank 45 Super Six-Four's copilot, killed Silver Star,*

*Air Medal with Valor Device, Purple Heart[68]*

*CW3 Clifton "Elvis" P. Wolcott 36 Super Six-One's*

*pilot, died in crash Distinguished Flying Cross,*

*Bronze Star,*

*Air Medal with Valor Device, Purple Heart[67]*

*CW3 Donovan "Bull" Briley 33 Super Six-One's copilot, died in crash Distinguished Flying Cross, Bronze Star,*

*Air Medal with Valor Device, Purple Heart[69]*

*Soldiers of the 2nd Battalion, 14th Infantry Regiment, 2nd Brigade, 10th Mountain Division*

*SGT Cornell Lemont Houston, Sr. 31 Killed on the rescue convoy Bronze Star with Valor Device,*

*de Fleury Medal, Purple Heart[70]*

*PFC James Henry Martin, Jr. 23 Killed on the rescue convoy Purple Heart"*

*For years I felt personally responsible for those deaths until I watched* the movie "Black Hawk Down[4]" and noted that General Garrison took responsibility for the blunder.

I still remember shedding tears as I watched the movie, and will always carry part of the responsibility, even though, I was not in a position to command and control the operation...

I was really upset about Clinton's policy that got the rangers killed. The media was starting to hype the situation; in my opinion journalist would rather write about war that prevent one.

Therefore, I called the Managing Editor Mike Dugan at Knight Rider News Service as they were huge and really hyping up potential conflict in Somalia. Knight Rider News Service is located in Washington, DC they had about thirty million daily readers.

---

[4] MOVIE credits; "Black Hawk Down"

I was convinced that Knight Rider wanted to engage in Yellow Journalism and provoke the situation in order to sell papers. I felt it important that I voice my concerns with the media giant...

I talked with Mr. Dugan at length on the phone sharing my experiences and his position still portrayed the Yellow Journalism opinions that I just mentioned.

I wasn't that fond of journalist anyway, they have a tendency to take good and distort it to bad at every opportunity. I have a bit of experience with that for sure...

Anyway, I let him know respectfully as possible that I didn't like to feel responsible for the deaths of those rangers because of the shifting policy of a missionary mission being converted to a military mission.

I also made the comment that they were just down the street from the President and that they had the influence on public opinion policy without putting pressure on the President to become a war President.

As the discussion got hotter and hotter, I also made a statement like "what the hells the matter with you folks are you in a coma or something" referring to their inability to realize the predicament, and the lives that they may cost by hyping up a conflict for no national security reason.

Just by coincidence the owner of Knight Rider News Service ended up in a car crash just down the street from the White House and slipped into a comma...Spooky hu... Perhaps a bit more divine intervention into my policy suggestions...

Summing up this chapter I had made the suggestion to my U.S. intelligence contacts that the United States should supply Aid to Somalia. American should sell it by having the press corps waiting on the coast as the troops came to shore.

*The media and the military...lol. This obviously wasn't a black ops and/or invasion operation with the press waiting for the military to arrive...*

*It still irritates me how Somalia turned bad with such silly militarization attempts by handlers and the press to make Clinton look like a real Commander and Chief... Or at least this is what I think his handlers had in mind when they allowed the shift in policy... Or perhaps General Garrison took it upon himself to make that shift as mentioned in the "Black Hawk Down[5]" movie credits.*

*After summing up, I will share some values, history and actions that I think are needed in Somalia and Africa... We clearly see that the military trying to do missionary missions is a problem. Yet, few NGO's have the stature to manage*

---

[5] MOVIE credits; "Black Hawk Down"

*missionary operations that require a security component.*

*Working in conjunction of supplying AID and Security is essential with the missionary taking the lead just as Diplomacy is the priority to prevent conflict.*

*To be able to do both, there has to be a more constructive U.N. involvement that creates huge "Green Zone" regions that provides missionary AID operations that are well secured. To include providing needed route be that air or vehicle security escort...*

*Reflecting back with a bit of sarcasm, I feel that the Catholic Church and/or a similar charity organization armed with a few agriculture tapes, made by the high school "Future Farmers of America" would have been more professional, and effective, than the military in supplying AID to Somalia.*

The military did not show maturity in this venture, nor was maturity in the Panama Invasion, or and war profiteering in the Gulf Region…

I still feel that Somalia sections off into various UN security and development sections to meet America's Constitutional Article 1 Section 8 to deal with Piracy. I would suggest diversifying the effort via the United Nations. Train and equip Military/Navel components and allow USAID, and the UN Development Program to do its job...

USAID and the UN could work more closely with Somalia Governors and the Centralized Government to develop a "Comprehensive Plan" to develop their communities and country. It would help them maintain a cohesive and comprehensive effort.

With a focus on creating, a bottom up "City/Rural Comprehensive Plan" to increased growth and development and *agricultural development Somalia will grow into a viable member of the World Community.*

*Somalia is a National Security and Humanitarian effort; however, there must be more focus on the appropriations of Somali tax base funding to ensure that agriculture, fishing, trade and commerce efforts to be maintained, and remain self sufficient...*

*Quick focus areas of interest would be; Trade and commerce collections going to fund agricultural efforts within the competitive market regions.*

*NOTE: The Corp of Engineers can clear large tracts of land for Agricultural access via roads just as well as Air bases, and Navel Bases to help establish more productive Port Cities, and to be able to respond to threats in the area.*

*If we spend more time educating the communities via "Comprehensive Planning" that provide tools for local,* state, and nation building. "Comprehensive Planning" spurs economic growth and long-term peace and prosperity tools, which adds real value to the in country relationship as well as their communities. "Comprehensive Planning" will gain more hearts and minds focused on Democracy and Development as opposed to Terror and Turmoil.

I strongly think that the 3D's will be required to keep peace and prosperity in focus in the future... Many joint ventures in key areas, perhaps even within the United States to develop infrastructure projects i.e. ring rail and roads around Key Cities to spur economic growth...

Diplomacy will require the military to make huge shifts in their mission statement. It will require a shift from full time warriors, to part time infrastructure developers under a New Earths Army.
The Militaries of the World "New Earths Army", Corp of Engineers and the like could work closely with the

*Department of State (USAID), and the UN Development Program and other like agencies from throughout the world to help build a more Peaceful and Prosperous World...*

# 4
# AFRICAN TERRORISM

*Deadly attacks in Somalia reflects failed polices from all involved, to include the United States...*

## U.S. Africa Command (AFRICOM)
**(The premier United States Military presence in the region asked the following question)**

*Verbatim text from this article link http://www.aljazeera.com/news/africa/2012/02/2012281556509078 41.html says "Al-Shabab claims Mogadishu car bombing." What effect do you think this armed Islamist movement has on other African nations? What actions do you think the U.S. and the western world could take to help instill stability in the regions affected!"*

*I think it is time to call "Al-Shabab" in for a meeting and discuss how "Destructive Leadership is spreading and becoming more popular than that of Constructive Leadership"... Ask them what is their agenda is? Ask if they really want to see destruction as apposed to construction...*

*Once you get a few "No's"; from the direct questions; then ask the simple questions... Ask if "Al-Shabab" and other Islamist Agenda's is not basically the same as the United States and that of the Western World to improve the economic and social conditions of Somalia?*

*I think you will get a "Yes" to that question and that will be good, as real changes will begin to occur once people realize that we all have Somalia's best interest at heart, but also look for strategic national security presence to protect the shipping lanes... Since we are there we can work together to make the region/Africa a much better place for it citizens and families...*

*The simple recognition of "Basic Human Rights" Citizen Involvement in improving communities, cities, and their nations will go a long way... As we all have ultimately the same goals and objectives for Somalia; however, we have all made mistakes...*

*We have to recognize our faults as well... We can start by recognizing the silliness of "Black Hawk Down", which converted a Missionary Mission into Military Mission, did little to help Somalia... Such operations would not have a place under new agreements with Al-Shabab's call for a non-violence policy...*

*Having been the guy that suggested the "Missionary Mission" to Somalia I am still shocked at how it got converted into a "Military Mission" that cost so many lives... Such operations have done little to build new and more constructive relations with Somalia?*

*I discussed a bit of my thoughts on how to improve AFRICOM relations and how to assist in the development of Africa via AFRICOM's questions.*

*Using those thoughts when Al-Shabab comes to the discussion table AFRICOM can discuss how working together to make a better Somalia is in the best interest of all involved and especially for the Somalia people...*

*"Al-Shabab" and others must bring their young men and women to the table to learn new trades and citizen involvement*

via *"Professional Public Administrators"*. *They must denounce violence and turn their Leadership skills that are so charismatic that young people will strap a bomb to themselves, or drive a suicide car bomb into a crowd of innocent people into something much more constructive for Somalia…*

*Al-Shabab's leadership can, and should be converted into something constructive for society. The United States State Department and AFRICOM has a huge role to play via the use of "Diplomatic" means. They have to be willing to invite groups to a secure table to recognize that everyone is fighting for the same thing (bettering Somalia). Once people recognize that, then such craziness will stop…*

*This craziness and destructiveness has been from both sides I might add…*

"*Black Hawk Down*" *and the conversion from a Missionary Mission to a Military Mission was just as ludicrous, and also sent young men on a gung ho "suicide mission."*

*I think anyone looking back and/or watching the "Black Hawk Down" move would certainly concluded that the operation was poorly planned and downright idiotic, and really did little to make real change for Somalia...*

*High School Future Farmers of America could have had a more profound effect on coming up with ways to feed the people in Somalia than a host of Generals and troops on the ground... This gung-ho attitude has to have some commonsense behind it...*

*Therefore, now that we all recognize faults and that we all have been trying to do good, but have resorted to silly and destructive means. Then we might be able to really find a way to deal with the real problems at hand…*

*Here is a draft "Comprehensive Plan/United Nations Global Reform Mandate*
*https://docs.google.com/viewer?a=v&pid=explorer&chrome=true&srcid=0B-ygIxNdW7E9YWE5NTBmNjMtZmY5OC00YmMyLThkNmUtNTc1MWJhMDVhM2Zj&hl=en_US*
*I promise if you try to bring more citizen involvement, to discuss real problems facing Somalia and not "BS"… It is time to discuss real growth, development and security concepts to improve Somali lives.*

*More and more will recognize that the U.S. is there to do some good as opposed to conflict… Yes, there will always be the need for security, but that security has to be constructive in nature and it should create growth and development in the region that would justify its existence...*

# 5
# UN BASE IN AFRICA

*Somalia should be cut into various UN security and development sections.*

*This would diversify the effort to train and equip Military/Navel components and allow USAID and the UN Development Program to do its job... USAID and the UN could work more closely with Somalia Governors and the Centralized Government to develop a "Comprehensive Plan" to develop their communities and country. It would help them maintain a cohesive and comprehensive effort.*

*With a focus on creating a bottom up "City/Rural Comprehensive Plan" to increased growth and development and agricultural development Somalia will grow into a viable member of the World*

Community. Somalia is a National Security and Humanitarian effort; however, there must be more focus on the appropriations of Somali tax base funding to ensure that agriculture, fishing, trade and commerce efforts are maintained and remain self sufficient...

Quick focus areas of interest would be; Trade and commerce collections going to fund agricultural efforts within the competitive market regions. NOTE: The Corp of Engineers can clear large tracts of land for Agricultural access via roads just as well as air bases to respond to threats in the area.

The military can avoid the blunders of the missionary conversion to a military mission that got 19 US Rangers Killed and about 3000 Somali's killed (according to the credits in the movie "Black Hawk Down."), by using simple commonsense.

*If the military don't have any ask a High School Future Farmer of America (FFA) they will tell you how to develop Agriculture programs without getting into a fight...*

*These Military Efforts and Corp of Engineers could work closely with the Department of State (USAID), and the UN Development Program and other like agencies from throughout the world...*

# 6
# AMERICA EXPANDS INFLUENCE

*America expanding economic influence into Africa and other Developing Nations... Africa has many, many thriving cities. It is not the Africa that kids watch on "National Geographic." It is vast with great market potential...*

*I strongly believe Africa can develop in a much more constructive way with America's USAID Assistance. Yet, the West has to get over the "National Geographic" version of Africa, and realize that Africa has nearly 1 billion people, and that Africa has many great cities and vast opportunities for American trade and commerce...*

*Africa on the other hand has to get over the thoughts that the West/America is only there to exploit Africa, when in actuality we are there like anywhere else to do business, and protect our investments...*

*Africa needs to realize that the Western Europeans, and America, has had a very constructive influence on the development of their economy. America enhanced the development of their cities for generations via trade and commerce. We can do much more in the future via more "Comprehensive Planning" that I will discuss in this paper...*

*America and Europe have a near $50,000 per capita income (PCI) as compared with Africa, which has (about $1,000 PCI with a few regions about 1/10$^{th}$ of the American PCI), India also (about $1,000 PCI), and China (about $4,000 PCI). Africa, China and India each have over 1 Billion people, and statistics as well as World Bank predictions all countries will continue to have very low PCI's for* decades to come… Due to their huge populations "Africa, India, China, they will also have a rise in a Middle Class Consumer that can purchase American Export Products, in a much more "Fair Trade Economy of Scale" type trading. This will be essential as America increases tariffs in the future to balance its trade deficit with these countries. Yet, there will still be great trade and commerce opportunities with America trading with Africa, India, China and so forth…

Unfortunately, as America struggles to reduce its trade imbalance with these countries dumping vast amounts of goods into the American Consumer Markets the Developing Nations will have economic difficulties…

Yet, we can be proactive and deal with America, the European Union and the Global Crises puts more stress on the Developing Nations… The solution is quite simple and quite necessary as it deals with the "Local Level" growth and development and the construction of infrastructure.

The solution will come in the form of training more "Professional Public Administrators" and getting local level citizens involved…

I strongly feel that America should continue USAID funding; however, that funding must joint venture with the United Nations Development Program and focus more on influencing "Technical Comprehensive Planning" such as this draft United Nations Global Reform Mandate to conduct city by city "Comprehensive Planning" https://docs.google.com/viewer?a=v&pid=explorer&chrome=true&srcid=0B-ygIxNdW7E9YWE5NTBmNjMtZmY5OC00YmMyLThkNmUtNTc1MWJhMDVhM2Zj&hl=en_US

*"Comprehensive Planning" and an open door policy to the West will increases local development, and attract Public-Private-Partnerships and the cooperation of Engineers, Builders, Investors/Land Developers, and Capital Markets from around the world to enhance local economies, build Industrial Parks, Rail, Roads, and other viable Infrastructure via Projects via Public-Private-Partnerships based on sound economic and finance principles...*

*As Africa and other developing nations gain success city by city, their nations and others around the World, gain value and can meet the needs of their citizens. Global Trade and Commerce opportunities will continue to feed, clothe and shelter citizens in more civilized way and with American type construction standards for TOWN HOMES, FLATS,*

*AND COMMERCIAL, RETAIL, HOTEL, AND OFFICE...*
*Attached:*
Draft USAID/United Nations Global Reform Mandate suggestion...

https://docs.google.com/viewer?a=v&pid=explorer&chrome=true&srcid=0B-yg1xNdW7E9YWE5NTBmNjMtZmY5OC00YmMyLThkNmUtNTc1MWJhMDVhM2Zj&hl=en_US

Africa could have far grander developments in the future via examples such as "The Venus Project"... and this more lengthy part 1 and part 2 http://www.youtube.com/watch?v=4Cu4qzDVjGQ. In addition, they have a website http://www.thevenusproject.com/.

My "Comprehensive Planning Tools and African Partnership Plans http://thesop.org/story/20120204/economic-powerhouse-america-spreads-its-influence-on-africa-and-other-3rd-world-

_nations.html_ _cannot solve all the issues;_ _however, I think the following can answer_ _the questions that you ask me_ "U.S. Africa Command (AFRICOM)      _Thanks_ _@Harvey Carroll for sharing this article._ _This article emphasizes the importance of_ _partnership between the west and African_ _nations. What effect would open-door_ _policy, developmental and security_ _training have on local development and_ _cross-border security?"_

# 7
# AFRICOM/USAID
# TECHNICAL/FUND

*An AFRICOM/USAID TECHNICAL/FUND can solve many of the economic and assist in dealing constrictively with the various African Border Issues...*

*You can look at any African country/border you wish; however, I would just mention that the Borders of Sudan because they have Oil Funding that could make such projects work, Somalia as they are of security concern and are of strategic shipping rout importance.*

*The violence flare ups in Nigeria which also has vast Oil funds to contributed to such projects. Lastly the reconstruction of Libya and Egypt; however, I think this will have to be a more AU/UN led mission to maintain a presence http://thesop.org/story/20120205/arab-*

_spring-turns-to-arab-winter-when-will-the-us-send-troops.html_ ...

One step closer at the African/Egypt Border is Israel and they have the opportunity to develop in a more constructive and peaceful manor as well _http://thesop.org/story/20120122/peace-park-and-my-two-state-solution-via-the-venus-project.html_

Is there, and will there continue to be a problem with Drugs, Guns, Black Market Goods and Illegal Immigration, and terrorism flowing across the various African Borders? YES; however, Diplomatic Relations between the United States and Africa can turn these economic, and immigration issues into something constructive, if we try...

So with that in the open, how can we provide jobs, opportunities that benefit American Foreign Policy, benefit Africa and deal with the various cross-border immigration and security issues... Keep immigrants from radicalizing and resorting to terrorism and/or crime that overpopulates jails...

How can poor African nations improve worker skills, and bridge language issues?

My solution is AFRICOM/USAID TECHNICAL/FUND could be a U.S., Africa Joint Venture, as well as a UN Development Project; whereby, worldwide capital market funds syndicated to develop vast growth projects throughout Africa.

Such programs could increase African labor opportunities, as well as spur economic development, and investment opportunities to increase jobs in America via trade and commerce...

Large scale projects focused on investing and building ring and railroads around key cities, perhaps metro's and/or railroads to key markets spurs growth and economic development... Perhaps build *new Cities in joint venture near key African borders like "The Venus Project" http://www.youtube.com/watch?v=gJfKXb vA5T8&feature=fvwrel and this more lengthy part 1 http://www.youtube.com/watch?v=DqplP -E8Dvw&feature=related and part 2 http://www.youtube.com/watch?v=4Cu4qz DVjGQ. In addition they have a website http://www.thevenusproject.com/.*

*New ring and rail projects provide many new sites for land developments such as office, logistics/industrial, apartments, housing communities as well as retail shops... Africa has the resources to build such facilities, they just need to be trained in understanding Professional Public Administration, as well as Land Development, and Finance...*

*A focus on a few key projects, cost analysis and the like could make such things more of a cookie cutter type process... It took me years to develop such skills after I got out of the Military and not* to show and disrespect to the Military, but most do not posses these capabilities either...

When they deploy they do so quickly and cost associated with such operations are usually not scrutinized... Defense spending climbed over 2 billion a day during the return to Iraq and the Afgan War, with very little to show for it in the form of real improvements to societies...

Alexander the Great hundreds of years ago still have more to show in the form of building cities and contributing to cultures via growth and development. Granted he did so by strong-arming, but he built and influenced the building of great cities...

I feel that American funds could and should have much more to show for our Foreign Policy expenditures and even gain a return on our hard working Taxpayer Dollars... AFRICOM working with USAID/UNDP could develop a mass *organized migrant open-door and/or cross-border worker/labor program concept where thousands of Africans are allowed to cross-borders and stay in "Infrastructure Development Camps."*

*Camps could develop infrastructure projects much like large scale Military/Corps of Engineer projects or the TVA "New Deal era" projects of the post Depression days...*

*AFRICOM knows such projects are possible. While in the Army, I used to participate in mass mobilization of tens of thousands of troops, and the rail heading of hundreds of tanks across Germany in just a few short hours...*

*Once there the mission went into effect. Some times that involved establishing temporary housing, and the building of roads, airfields, and so forth... Now entire Military Cities have been developed to accomplish military missions, such as in Iraq and Afghanistan...*

Therefore, I think it is reasonable to use the same concept to successful develop mass infrastructure projects throughout Africa in and around key cities and/or borders... Here is the basic concept of more developed housing as the plan progresses. Rail Road or low cost prefab or tent housing; (I am not talking about the WWII Cattle Cars filled with slave labor and would be appalled to think that projects would not be grand enough in scale to show real pride by those that are given a job). I am talking about decent mobile housing that can be railed into areas, and/or trucked/airlifted in and set up.

This mobile housing can establish jobs for African workers. Such mobile labor movement can add real value by developing African infrastructure projects that will spurs growth and development in all facets of the economy. These mobile employment camps would supply reasonable wages in safe and secure surroundings, as well as provide respect *and pride in U.S./Africa relations, instead of disputes over border issues...*

*Before, people start thinking this is silly. I again remind you that the American Military and the U.N. has built mobile cities in Iraq and Afghanistan using Military forces, and contract labor to build infrastructure in those areas today...*

*So, why would it not work in Africa as well? All while increasing America's investments in Africa, providing new Tax Base Jobs for Cross Cultural Workers, and Americans alike, as well as creating investment opportunities for World Wide Capital Markets in Key City and/or Border Projects...*

# 8
# AFRICAN FAITH ISSUES AND ECONOMICS

*My pondering thoughts of American/Global Economics and Peace on Christmas, as a response to the Nigerian Christian Church bombings...*

*I as most Christians do on Christmas think of and wish the best for our family and friends and their families... Then we give a quick thought to Peace in the World... Folks like us give probably most of the day's attention to those thoughts and perhaps even neglect family and friends while lost in thoughts...*

*Obviously, millions of people's attention was directed towards Nigeria's Christian Church bombings "terrorism"... I am sure that most like myself initially had thoughts of anger and feeling that the Christians should be armed to be able to protect themselves just go to Worship God; the same god that those that wish to destroy Christians believe in... Therefore, my thoughts then went from anger to thinking of the old Christian saying of turning the other cheek as retaliation only brings more violence to the region...*

*I always follow the money trial and quickly review the thoughts of special interest as "Terrorism in many ways has converted to Corporate-Sponsored Terrorism, as opposed to State Sponsored Terrorism"... Therefore, I kicked around the idea of primary American Oil Contractors in Nigeria and what role they play in religions, political and business practices within the country, region and the World...*

*I concluded that Corporate-Sponsored Terrorism is extreme; however, they are like any special interest and would propose a "Bill" or law that self-serves over* the interest of the host or native countries people.

Yet, I saw no direct link of any Corporate-Sponsored Terrorism, but did have thoughts that many would seek to manipulate the minds of the masses for personal profit. I have come to realize that such parasitic profiteers (be it the Defense industry or Anti-American sects throughout the World) would obviously use religion as a way to get America to engage in Defense Activities in Nigeria, or anywhere else; such as in the dealing with Israel and now Iran... This is obviously disturbing as Religion goes beyond a small fray and brings in multitudes in seconds...

Then my thoughts turned to a grander view of Africa. First, and foremost my thoughts of Africa go far beyond the child hood TV shows of Wild Kingdom and/or National Geographic versions of Africa. Africa has nearly 1 Billion People *and has many very large Cities just like the rest of the World…*

*To give you more of my general view of Africa I considered three concepts such as (Religious, Political and Business) concepts, and then divided Africa into three regions (North Africa, Central Africa and South Africa)… I took into account the predictions of the World Bank to realize that decade from now that Africa as a whole will only have a GDP Per-Capita Income (PCI) of just a bit over $1,000 dollars. Obviously, this makes it difficult to export and/or do equal trade and commerce as the United States has a near $46,000 PCI…*

*NORTH AFRICA- In a triangle view of North Africa we see that Incomes range from less than $3,000 to a peek of about $15,000 in Libya. Obviously, Libya has been an important Oil Exporter to the United States and mainly across the*

Mediterranean Sea to our NATO *friends* in Western Europe.

I think Morocco (<$3000 PCI), Algeria (<$5000 PCI), Libya ($15,000 PCI), and Egypt (<$5,000 PCI). While the Muslim religion is the predominate religion, we have not seen vast displays of radical extremism; I think that radical extremism is not prevalent in the Arabic regions of North Africa because they are not isolated societies in that they have daily dealings with the West.

Business wise they have come to rely on the economic trade and commerce as well as the multi-million dollar tourism trade from the United States and our NATO Allies. The Countries that border the Coastal Countries and the Countries mentioned above on the contrary began to take a drastic Per Capita-Income (PCI) drop, as they become much more isolated from the West; yet depend on much of the *trade and commerce of their Northern neighbors...*

Yet, their PCI's in general are only about ($400 PCI), with the Persian Gulf "Divided State of Sudan" topping the PCI chart of about ($1,500 PCI)... They, as well as the countries bordering them to the North are predominantly Muslim; yet, I think that they have a tendency to abandon radical Islam as their business relationships depend on their northern neighbor's relationships with the West...

CENTRAL AFRICA- As isolationism from the West increases (excluding Oil imports from a few American contractors), we also see the amount of Poverty and vast drops in Per Capita Incomes (PCI) to less than $1,000 dollars... We have seen radical extremism in Nigeria (<$1,400 PCI) with a population of nearly 150 Million in the Western part of Central Africa with the recent Christmas day Church bombings, as well as radical extremism in Somalia (<$300 PCI) on the Eastern Coast of the Central Africa "Horn of Africa."

Nigeria is about 50/50 Muslim to Christian and Somalia of course is predominantly. I see that the extremism is of course more economic than that of Muslim vs Christian. The attacks on the shipping lanes along the Somali Coast are primary Pirating and the quest for financial gain, as opposed to disrupting shipping lanes for a grand religious purpose. I also see that Somalia is in disarray and has been for decades as they fight fellow Muslims over resources to survive and not over religion...

SOUTHER AFRICA- As we journey to the south we see more and more equal 50/50 Muslim to Christian percentages and we see PCI's remain low of about a ($1,000); with only a few countries prospering in the region due to more Trade and Commerce with the West. Such as Equatorial Guinea (27,000 PCI), Gabon ($10,000 PCI), and South Africa (<$7,000)...

As I start to conclude I recognize that Africa (about $1,000 PCI), India also (about $1,000 PCI), and China (about $4,000 PCI) has very low PCI's... China, India, and Africa as a whole all have a 1 Billion people each and statistics as well as World Bank predictions all countries will continue to have very low PCI's; however, due to their huge populations they will also have a rise in a Middle Class Consumer that can purchase American Export Products...

The perplexing issue is how can America with a $46,000 PCI, can produce diversify and target the people that are wealthy enough to purchase our products, while also producing cheap enough to open *up trade and commerce with the masses of Africa and India with a $1,000 Per Capita Income, and China's ($4,000 PCI) in a way that the United States maintains strength in its Dollar and maintains American standards and way of life...*

*A few thoughts on this are;*

1) *Continue Christian Missionaries as President Obama's mother and father did in Kenya.*
2) *Continue to focus on developing and understanding trade and commerce with the World.*
    a. *fund this by raising import tariffs to protect American internal jobs, and be able to fund Defense, State and Commerce Department activities...*
3) *Continue to discuss and justify tariffs over free trade due to currency manipulation and the*

*exploitation of human rights, child labor and other labor standards, which are being abused in these developing countries... Many of which are many times worse than the American Prison Populations are producing license plates and such.*

*Zambia has past ties with the UK. Since the roaring 20's mining has been a staple, but not without roller coaster ups and downs with copper prices. In the 90's a one party rule sparked a number of corruption case. Zambia got debt relief that helped in some economic growth opportunities.*

*Koroma, aided in the peace process of Sierra Leone's anti-corruption that established a "Business Zone" to improve infrastructure and investments.*

My *"Comprehensive Planning"* tool and *"Professional Public Administrator"* training should…

Professional Public Administrator:

https://docs.google.com/fileview?id=0B-ygIxNdW7E9MWRmNWNlYWItMDA4ZC00NDhmLWI1MDYtZGFjNWU2MzQwZDhh&hl=en&authkey=CKnziIEB

Comprehensive Plan:
https://spreadsheets.google.com/ccc?key=0AuygIxNdW7E9dFlrS3VOWmgwbXJwQWNNOVpaNzBPckE&hl=en&authkey=CKKqj5gP

# 9
# AFRICAN CONCLUSIONS

*Here are some suggestions of what I think might help. There is a need for UN to cut Somalia into districts for Navel Bases to patrol and protect the shipping lanes from Pirates and perhaps help the regions develop their economies via "Comprehensive Planning" (I have such tools available if needed) and the development of their agricultural base.*

*The invention of plows, and disk that can be connected to a trailer hitch would go a long way in tilling the land for planting...*

*Bill Gates and others have hosted forums on developing ag projects and feeding people they might get involved in helping design the ag plows to reduce famine.*

# SOMALIA "BLACK HAWK DOWN"
## My Missionary Mission turned Military Mission
### (THE UNELECTED PRESIDENT)
### By
### Harvey Carroll, Jr.

I'm a former U.S. Army Military Policeman/Investigator turned high level political consultant that has dealt with the Panama Invasion "Operation Just Cause", organizing the 1st Gulf War "Operation Desert Storm" and my third International Affairs venture was suggesting the missionary mission into Somalia turned military mission; hence "Black Hawk Down."

I now hold a Bachelors of Business Administration Degree specializing in Real Estate and Finance, and three partial Masters in Business, Public Administration as well as Diplomacy and International Commerce...

I've been considered the most influential international political figure in Kentucky-US, and some would say that perhaps in the World at one time. I have dealt with Governors, Senators, Presidents and Foreign Heads of State; and in the process I have saved millions of lives, and affected the economic fate of nations... Yet, I have made mistakes, and even cost lives and often ponder if the "End Justified the Means."

It has always been quite easy for me to deal with complex U.S. National and International Policy. From a young age I dealt with local, state, national and international policy that includes Latin America i.e. "Panama," Middle East (Iraq, Libya, Syria, Israel, Iran), Africa, and even coming to the AID after the collapse of the Soviet Union to protect U.S. and Global Security by suggesting buying out the nuclear weapons to prevent them from ending up on the Black Market for Terrorism, as well as preventing the former fifteen Soviet States against each other.

I also suggested financial bailouts, and another financial AID via the IFC/World Bank for Ukraine that saved seventy-five banks a few years ago (a similar plan presented to the U.S. House and Senate Financial Services Committee "Frank and Dodd" to bailout the American Economy to assist 2/3rds of the American States and Top Banks from Collapse.

More recently, I have shared suggestions to have the OSCE get between the separatist and the Ukrainian Army to the Ukrainian Presidents people tasked to negotiate the Minsk Agreements that may have prevented Ukraine from turning into another Syria... In the process I have noticed that Russian President Putin sent Troops "Little Green Men" into Crimea; thereby, leading me to offer up a "Crimean Compromise."